Brooks B. Robinson

A BlackEconomics.org
MONOGRAPH

JEL Codes: Z120, J150, O150

BlackEconomics.org®
P.O. Box 8848
Honolulu, HI 96830
www.BlackEconomics.org
BlackEconomics@BlackEconomics.org

Dedication

To future generations of Afrodescendants who will learn to use all tools at their disposal to resolve Afrodescendant issues.

Preface

"Talk is cheap! It takes money to buy land."

The just-given famous adage emphasizes an important fact: One can engage in eternal verbosity; however, more often than not, one must expend material resources to transform material circumstances. In this monograph, we discuss Afrodescendants' unwillingness to "buy land." Specifically, we examine the apparent failure of Afrodescendants to use a clear, effective, and available tool to motivate improvements in our economic circumstances—contemporary Gospel Music. Quite frankly, we call into question our own integrity when we elaborate the issues that confront Afrodescendants, but then refuse to use means that are at our disposal to resolve those issues.

We often cite the Black Church as the most important institution in the Black community. In doing so, we may overlook the fact that the church is a multifaceted institution. The preachers/pastors, no doubt, play key roles. However, the musical component of the liturgy is integral to establishing the tone for service and preparing the membership for the message. More importantly, technology and consumer demand have taken Gospel Music far beyond the four walls of the church edifice. Today, you can hear Gospel Music everywhere you go.

As a melting pot of African rhythms, the Spirituals, Blues, Jazz, Rock, Soul, Reggae, Rap, Hip-Hop, and Electronic Music, Gospel Music includes a defining note for everyone. Therefore, contemporary Gospel Music is an easily available tool that can be used to influence outcomes in our community. We should not forget that, in the 1960s during the Civil Rights struggle, most musical *genres* were redirected in some way toward the cause. Gospel Music was not the least of these as lyrics of Gospel songs were altered to produce, among other things, "Freedom Songs."

Consequently, the important question to ask today is why isn't more Afrodescendant music (including contemporary Gospel Music) directed at helping drive more favorable outcomes for our community—especially, economic outcomes?

This monograph does not answer this important question because only the artists can truly answer it. However, the monograph contains an analysis that proves the absence of a focused and vigorous effort to use Gospel Music as a tool to create positive change for Afrodescendants.

Ultimately, we must all answer the question in that GREAT DAY when we are asked: "What did you do to improve Afrodescendants' plight?

Did you start a new business in order to create change? Did you protect and teach the children in order to create change? Did you organize the community in order to create change? Did you seek to establish a separate nation, which may be the only realistic solution for Afrodescendants' problems in America?"

Many will say: "I prayed."

HE will say: "Talk is cheap. It takes money to buy land."

.

Table of Contents

I.   Introduction

United States (US) Afrodescendants' position at the lower-end of economic metrics in the US was reinforced during the Great Recession of 2008-2009.[1] Social groups in such a position are expected to use all available resources to improve their plight—including religion. A key component of the Afrodescendant religious tradition (in and outside of religious liturgies) is Gospel Music. No question about it, Gospel Music has been used historically as a motivating force for improving conditions for Afrodescendants. Did Afrodescendants use Gospel Music to improve their economic condition in response to the Great Recession? More broadly, what are the discernable effects of contemporary Gospel Music? This monograph reflects findings from musical, content, and Probit regression analysis of contemporary Gospel Music. We find that, while economic concerns are strongly present in the Gospel Music exchange, the medium is not widely used to motivate improved economic outcomes for Afrodescendants.

This monograph unfolds as follows. In Section II, we provide context by discussing the theoretical relationship between economics and religion and the role of Gospel Music in that relationship. In Section III, we examine the psychological impact of contemporary Gospel Music by providing a musical analysis. In Section IV, we dig deep into the nature of contemporary Gospel Music by presenting a content analysis, which describes the music's ability to affect economic outcomes for Afrodescendants through its lyrics. In Section V, we explore and test statistical relationships between Gospel Music and key economic and

---

[1]By Afrodescendant we mean those persons who find themselves in the US mainly due to the selling or trading of Africans to Europeans, who brought the former to the Western Hemisphere to serve as slaves. Henceforth, we will simply refer to Afrodescendants.

noneconomic variables in order to develop an understanding concerning the use of Gospel Music to enhance economic outcomes for Afrodescendants. The results of our statistical analysis are presented in Section VI. Section VII provides a summary and conclusion. Section VIII presents references.

II.　　Economics, Religion, and Gospel Music

As a scene setter, we must first establish that religion, which is part of culture, can affect economic outcomes. Second, we must provide a model of the church, which is the prime purveyor of religion within culture. Third, we must make the connection between the church model and the cultural phenomenon about which we are concerned (i.e., Gospel Music), and explain how that cultural phenomenon can affect economic outcomes.

Guiso, Sapienza, and Zingales (2006) answer the question, "Does Culture Affect Economic Outcomes?" Their answer describes the impact of culture on beliefs, expectations, and preferences, and then shows how those beliefs, expectations, and preferences affect economic outcomes. A key cultural factor that is used to complete this proof is trust. The authors discuss how the level of trust that exists in a society is largely culturally determined. They go on to make the link between culture and economics by arguing that high trust levels (part of a system of beliefs) are sufficient to produce vibrant economic outcomes—more so than low trust levels. The authors cite Arrow (1972), Knack and Keefer (1996), and Knack and Zak (2001) to confirm this tight relationship between trust and favorable economic outcomes.

It is common knowledge that religious customs/culture is transmitted from generation to generation mainly through churches or similar institutional arrangements. Churches, as institutions, can be modeled in several ways (Iannaccone,

1998). Following Stark and Bainbridge (1985) and Dolin, Slesnick, and Byrd (1989), we choose to model churches as firms that seek to optimize profits. Specifically, churches are expected to optimize the following function:

Equation 1:
$$max: \pi = R - C$$

Where π is the universal symbol for profits, R is for revenues, and C is for costs. Below, we expand the R and C arguments of the function:

Equation 2:
$$R = R(E, I, G, FR, O(sMW, sEP))$$

Equation 3:
$$C = C(FC, VC)$$

The variables for the R argument of the function (Equation 2) are a church's endowment (E), inheritances (I), gifts (G), returns from fund raising (FR) efforts, and offerings (O), which are comprised of a share of church members' wages (sMW) and/or a share of church members' entrepreneurial profits (sEP). In Equation 3, we keep the cost argument (C) simple by reflecting two broadly defined variables: Churches' fixed costs (FC) and variable costs (VC).

We place this profit maximizing church firm in the context of Afrodescendant denominations that reflect loose relationships between central organizations and individual churches (BlackEconomics.org, 2013).[2] In addition, there

_____

[2] The cited report brief chronicles the nature of the loose relationship between individual Afrodescendant and white churches and central authorities. In this case, central authorities had very scanty information concerning the number and average value of college scholarships that were extended by individual churches each year. It stands to reason

are many "stand-alone" Afrodescendant churches that have no ties to central bodies whatsoever. In either case, preachers/pastors of these independent or pseudo-independent churches act as entrepreneurs—competing with other preachers/pastors for members. The entrepreneur preacher/pastor is motivated to maximize profits. Therefore, given some set of *FC, VC, E,* and *I* that we will assume to be given, the entrepreneur preacher/pastor can maximize profits by expending efforts to attract gifts (*G*) and to optimize fund raising (*FR*) and offerings (*O*).[3] For the latter, the entrepreneur preacher/pastor will maximize profits when all members are earning wages or capturing entrepreneurial profits and are contributing a share of those earnings and profits as offerings. In this scenario, it appears reasonable that the entrepreneurial preacher/pastor would use every tool available to stimulate unemployed members to become employed and earn wages and/or to engage in entrepreneurial efforts to earn profits. While the spoken word (sermon) is clearly one of those tools, we will build the argument below that Gospel Music has the capacity to serve as one of these tools also.

Nathaniel Frederick II (2009) contends that the history of Gospel Music begins in the 1930s; promulgated by the writing and works of Charles Albert Tindley and Thomas Andrew Dorsey. It evolves from Afrodescendants' sacred music—Spirituals—and secular music—Jazz and the Blues. The great preacher, historian, and musicologist, Wyatt Tee Walker (1979), says: "Gospel music, at bottom, is religious folk music that is clearly identifiable with the social circumstance of the Black community in America." What

---

that central authorities have weak reins on individual churches in other aspects of the relationship.

[3] Specifically, we assume that adopting or expanding contemporary Gospel Music into church liturgies imposes no additional variable costs than would otherwise exist.

4

we know is that, at a minimum, Gospel Music is the embodiment of Afrodescendant musical expression of the complex struggle and pain of what it means to be Black in America, while yet holding out the prospect of joy that is promised in the overcoming of it all. History tells us that it is even more. According to Webster (2011), who researched Gospel Music's survival, elevation, and liberation themes, Gospel Music has also been a motivator for Afrodescendants by incorporating prescriptions for change.

Gospel Music serves as a musical component of religious liturgies that creates an ambiance for the spoken word component of the liturgy. In Afrodescendant churches, Gospel Music often sets the tone for preachers' messages. Preachers and choir directors coordinate their presentations to optimize the mood and tone that they plan to evoke. If the preacher plans to provide an inspiring, uplifting sermon, then the choir can facilitate the preacher's effort by presenting uplifting, joyous Gospel Music. The reverse is also true. For example, for funerals or other somber occasions, the Gospel Music that is presented prior to and after eulogies are often of a somber or melancholy nature.

As already indicated, and like other *genres* of mainly popular music, Gospel Music has served as "message music." For example, the 1960's saw the development of Gospel songs (in this case called "Freedom Songs") that not only set the tone for, but, in fact, helped drive the Civil Rights Movement: e.g., "I Ain't Gonna Let Nobody Turn Me Around"; "Keep Your Eyes on the Prize"; "We Shall Overcome"; and "We Shall Not Be Moved" (Norris, 2013). Consequently, in the midst of adverse economic conditions that were exacerbated by the Great Recession of 2008 and 2009, one might expect message music on economic topics to pervade Gospel Music and serve as motivation for Afrodescendants to improve their outcomes. This

5

expectation takes on more meaning when we consider our model of the Afrodescendant church as a profit maximizing firm. We will explore this issue further as part of our content analysis after we have presented a musical analysis.

III.   Musical Analysis

For now, we focus on Gospel Music's ability to motivate positive and upbeat versus sad or somber emotions. Dalla Bella *et al* (2001), Gagnon and Peretz (2003), Hunter, Schellenberg, and Shimmack (2008 and 2010), and Rigg (1937) are among a plethora of scholars who build strong evidence on the psychological effects of music. They verify or confirm the idea that music that is presented at fast tempi and in a major musical key engenders stronger happy emotions/feelings among listeners than music that is presented at slow tempi and in a minor musical key. In addition, most of these scholars suggest that musical tempo and mode produce the following general happy-to-sad emotional spectrum: Fast tempi/Major key (most happy); Fast tempi/Minor key (second most happy); Slow tempi/Major key (third most happy); and Slow tempi/Minor key (lowest level of happiness).

Therefore, we asked: "What emotions are generated by contemporary Gospel Music?" We gathered the Top 25 Gospel Songs as presented by *Billboard* magazine over the years 2008 – 2013 and conducted a musical analysis with respect to the songs' tempi and musical key.[4,5] Following Hunter, Schellenberg, and Shimmack (2010), we established

---

[4]We begin our analysis with 2008 because it is the first year that *Billboard* magazine initiated its reporting of the Top 25 Hot Gospel Songs.
[5]This musical analysis was conducted by James Morford during December of 2013. Morford was a doctoral degree candidate at the University of Washington in Seattle, Washington.

90 beats per minute (BPM) as the line of demarcation between slow and fast musical pieces, and we identified the musical key of each of the 150 songs.

We found that 66 (44%) of the 150 songs reflected 90 BPM or higher, and that 117 (78%) of the 150 songs were recorded in a major musical key. Forty-six of the fast songs were recorded in major musical keys, while 20 of the fast tempi songs were recorded in minor keys. Of the 84 songs that reflected less than 90 BPM, 71 were in a major key. Only 13 of the slow tempi songs were recorded in a minor key. Therefore, we conclude that an overwhelming majority (91%) of the 150 songs included in our analysis were of a tempi and tonal configuration to produce greater than the lowest level of happiness (songs of slow tempi and recorded in a minor key; see Chart 1).

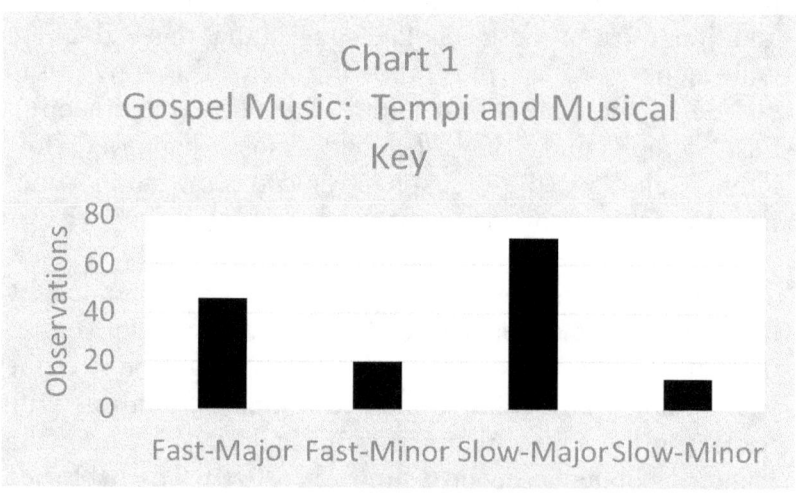

From a purely musical perspective, these findings reveal that the most popular contemporary Gospel Music can engender upbeat, happy feelings among its listeners. Whether these listeners hear this Gospel Music in church environments, on traditional or Internet radio or television stations, or at

7

Gospel Music concerts, they are likely to come away with happy feelings. Theoretically, these happy sentiments cause listeners to feel good about themselves. Such feelings bode well for preachers who leverage those feelings when building their sermons, and follow it all up with collection of an offering. If those good feelings have been optimized, then offering collection are likely to be optimized.

Considering these Gospel Music-motivated happy feelings from an economic perspective, how do they affect listeners' willingness to act to improve their economic outcomes? Do the happy feelings stimulate increased work effort, increased efforts to capture employment, or efforts to initiate entrepreneurial activities? *Ceteris paribus*, a positive or happy feeling should stimulate each of the aforementioned efforts. However, if we assume that the Afrodescendant population has long-standing and ongoing exposure to Gospel Music and that the music has always been generally configured to motivate happy feelings, then there is no reason to believe that Afrodescendants would enhance their economic efforts during or following the Great Recession.

On the other hand, if the musical component of Gospel Music is accompanied by lyrics that have a special message that motivates improvements in economic outcomes under the unique circumstances of the Great Recession, then we might expect contemporary Gospel Music to have a positive effect on Afrodescendants' economic conditions. What is the evidence that special Gospel Music lyrics (messages) can motivate adherents to improve their economic conditions?

Borghans *et al* (2008) and Cunha and Heckman (2007) support the idea that personality traits can be changed by environmental factors—including changes in social roles. Moreover, Roberts, Helson, and Klohnen (2002) show that personality trait changes are most enduring when the factors

8

that influence the change are substantive and permanent, such as when an individual marries and becomes part of a family. One might argue that when adherents join religious organizations they are, in fact, joining a family. Therefore, to the extent that adherents remain in a religious organization, the environmental change is permanent and the personality change may be enduring. Finally, according to Borghans *et al* (2008), personality change is effected most easily before the passing of young adulthood. Notably, it is young adult Afrodescendants who experience the highest levels of unemployment and who can be motivated by Gospel Music with motivating lyrics. In other words, we hypothesize that Afrodescendants, particularly young adults, may be motivated to take action to improve their economic circumstances when they are part of religious institutional arrangements and engage in regular listening to Gospel Music that includes appropriately designed motivating (special) messages.[6]

Do the 150 most popular Gospel songs that we analyzed contain such special messages? What would be the nature of such messages? We explore these questions in the next section.

IV.   Content Analysis

To determine whether Gospel Music includes special messages, we conducted a content analysis of the aforementioned 150 selections to: (1) Categorize the songs; (2) determine whether economic issues/topics were

---

[6]As an indicator of Gospel Music's potential reach, the Gospel Music Association (2007) reported that over 900 radio stations in the nation broadcast Christian Music, and that over 20 million Americans listen to Christian/Gospel Music stations each week. In addition, the Nielsen Company (2013) reports that 92% of Black Americans listen to radio each week.

entertained in the songs; and (3) identify the existence of specific motivating messages in the songs. By categorize, we mean classifying the songs according to their major lyrical themes. By "economic issues," we mean lyrics that reference finances; business; jobs or working conditions; a dearth of money or insufficient resources; and the like. By "motivating messages," we mean lyrics that include positive action words concerning an individual's or a group's ability to overcome difficult hardships or unfavorable situations. We constrained the latter messages to be extended directly to individuals or groups without immediate, concomitant references to "God," "Jesus," or "the Lord." We established this constraint to ensure that the message is one of a self-empowering nature. In other words, we sought in these songs the type of lyrics that conveyed to listeners that they could overcome adverse economic conditions through their own effort without reliance on magical relief, which is caused by a deity or deity-driven forces.

We categorized the 150 songs based on the major lyrical themes that were embodied in the songs (see Table 1 for the categories and related descriptions). Fifty-one (34%) of the songs reflected "praise." Twenty-eight (18.6%) of the songs espoused "faith." Twenty-two (14.7%) of the songs expressed "victory." Sixteen (10.7%) of the songs reflected "requests." Fifteen (10%) of the songs expressed "worship." The remaining songs embodied the following themes: "Instruction," "thanks," "joy," "love," "confession," "encouragement," and "realization." As expected, this categorization shows that the lyrics of the songs mainly reflected religious-oriented themes. It was somewhat surprising to find a significant number of the songs expressing victory—although most of these victories were related to religious, not economic, issues. Consequently, this aspect of the content analysis ushered up no startling evidence concerning the use of contemporary Gospel

Music's most popular songs to resolve Afrodescendants economic issues.

Table 1.—Contemporary Gospel Music Categories

Line No.	Categories	Number of Songs	Descriptions
1	Confession	1	Song concerns a confession to God
2	Faith	28	Song concerns an expression of faith and of God's ability to effect life changes
3	Encouragement	1	Song encourages adherents that God will resolve issues
4	Instruction	6	Song provides instructions to adherents
5	Joy	2	Song concerns an expression of joy—for God's goodness
6	Love	2	Song concerns expression of love for God
7	Praise	51	Song concerns praise for God
8	Realization	1	Song expresses a realization about God
9	Request	16	Song concerns a request to God
10	Thanks	5	Song expresses thanks to God
11	Victory	22	Song claims victory over life's problems with and without God's direct intervention
12	Worship	15	Song is an actual worship effort
13	**Total**	**150**	

Our content analysis revealed that 46 (31%) of the 150 songs included lyrics with references to economic issues. This indicates that almost one out of three of the most popular Gospel Music songs made at least a passing reference to economic issues during 2008 – 2013. Clearly, economic issues were an important concern to song writers during this period. The important follow-up question is, "Did those same song writers analyze the economic issues and suggest methods for resolving the economic issues?" Given that

Gospel Music song writers are not economists, a more reasonable question to ask is, "Were lyrical references to economic issues accompanied by lyrics that were designed to encourage or motivate listeners to overcome their economic hardships?"

It turns out that only 10 (6.7%) of the 150 songs included lyrics of a "motivating message" nature. The following lists reflects the 10 songs with excerpted lyrics that represent "motivating messages":[7]

1. "Livin" by The Clark Sisters (2008): "I can speak to mountains. They will be moved. I can speak to dreams. They will come true."
2. "Declaration (This is It)" by Kirk Franklin (2008): "If you are a survivor, get up; stand up and fight."
3. "My Name is Victory" by Jonathan Nelson (2008): "I've got confidence. I'm a conqueror. I know that I win. My name is victory."
4. "Hold On" by Yolanda Adams (2008): "No matter how hard it seems, hold on to your dream. You are facing adversity, you can be on your feet. Determination is the key. In this cold world, if you are going to succeed. There is nothing you can't do. Don't be discouraged by the trials you face."
5. "Every Prayer" by Israel Houghton & Mary Mary (2009): "Hold on. While you are waiting, encourage yourself. Hold on. You can make it."
6. "Walking" by Mary Mary (2010): "Look at me. I'm trying. Everyday. I fall down. Make mistakes. Get back up. Try again."

---

[7]The song lyrics were confirmed mainly using websites cited under "Song Lyrics" in the References.

7. "God Made Me" by the Mississippi Mass Choir (2010): "I am a conqueror. I am victorious. I can't be blocked. I can't be stopped. I am an achiever."
8. "Survive" by Mary Mary (2011): "I encourage you to hold on. You will survive. Keep your head up and survive."
9. "Fly Again" by Jamecia Bennett and Sounds of Blackness (2011): "You've got to know that you will fly again…You've got to know that you will rise again…You hold the key to your victory."
10. "If He Did It Before" by Tye Tribbett (2013): "I won't give in. No, I'm not gone turn around. I know I win…I may fall. May get knocked down to the ground. But I know I'll rise up."

If the above listed songs with their motivating messages were more prevalent, we would have strong grounds for arguing that religious adherents who listen regularly to these songs could experience a personality trait changes—including expending efforts to improve their economic circumstances. Ten such songs out of 150 songs over a six-year period may not, however, constitute sufficient prevalence.

Given the prevalence of economic issues in the most popular contemporary Gospel Music over the past six years, it seemed anomalous that so few songs attempted to motivate listeners to overcome their economic problems. It was more common to find strong lyrical references to reliance on the power of God to resolve economic and all other types of problems—in a magical way without any direct action on the part of the individual. We found that at least 18 (12% of the 150 songs) songs reflected explicit lyrical references to reliance on "God," "Jesus," or "the Lord," to resolve problems/concerns—again, in a magical way without any effort (other than belief) on the part of religious adherents.

Several additional songs out of the 150 included less explicit, yet implied, lyrics that called for reliance on God. Excerpted lyrics from selected songs that invite listeners to rely solely on God are provided below:[8]

- "Still Able" by James Fortune and FIYA (2011): "If you lose your job... Everything... And you can't pay your bills... That you need...No food on the table... Everything... I know he's able... That you need...You can wipe your tears... Everything...Cause he's everything... That you need..."
- "God's Got It" by J Moss (2012): "I ain't gonna worry bout' the money in the bank, I ain't worried bout it. I ain't gonna worry bout' the gas in the tank, fill me up, fill me up, I ain't worried bout' it. I ain't gonna worry bout' the things I can't control, it is, what it is. I ain't worry bout' it, all I do is pray about it, hold up, why? God's got it..."
- "I've Seen Him Do It" by Kurt Carr & the Kurt Carr Singers (2012): "Whatever problem you've got. If you just give it to God, he'll work it out. How do I know? I've seen him do it. I've seen him do it"
- "Always" by Jason Champion-Brooks (2008): "Don't you worry about a thing tonight. I promise you that everything is gonna be alright. Hold your head up high, look up to the sky. Everything is gonna be alright."
- "They that Wait" by Fred Hammond and John P Kee (2009): "Hold on a little while longer. Here's what you got to do. Trust and believe my friend. He'll work it out for you...Wait on the Lord and he will come through. Wait on the Lord, he will answer you."

---

[8]Ibid.

14

- "Wait on the Lord" by Donnie McClurkin and Karen Clark-Sheard (2009): "Trust in the word of God. For His word is true. When did He promise anything in your life that He would not do. Trust and depend on Him. He's always on time. Don't be discouraged. If you just believe, you will receive it."
- "Resting on His Promises" by Youthful Praise featuring J Hairston (2009): "My Father promised to supply all my needs. With His riches in glory, He gives seed to the barren and food in famine. So I know that He'll take care of me. Jireh, is who He is. Providing is what He does. He won't let me lack, won't let me beg. Cause I'm His child, and He loves me…Go to sleep at night. Don't worry. Doors will be opened that you thought were closed. Put your mind at ease cause your father will never leave you nor forsake you."

The foregoing seven examples highlight prevalent lyrics in Gospel Music that advise adherents that they do not have to take action to improve their circumstances (economic or otherwise) or resolve their issues. They are told that God will work it out or resolve the issue. These are countervailing lyrics to the type of motivating messages that we have already discussed. In this latter case, we cannot expect listeners of these songs to experience a personality change that is directed at improving their economic conditions.

Given our interest in the hypothesis that Gospel Music with motivating messages can precipitate personality trait changes that produce improved economic outcomes, we developed an econometric (Probit regression) model to test relationships between the existence of such music and economic- and noneconomic-related variables that are relevant to the period of analysis (2008 - 2013). We present the model and explore its results in the next two sections.

V.　　Probit Analysis

We developed a Probit regression panel data model to explore statistical relationships between the 150 top Gospel Music songs over the past six years and covariates that are relevant to the songs' potential for motivating Afrodescendants to improve their economic outcomes. We selected a Probit model because, as Maddala (1987) suggests, our intent is to use the model to make inferences about the broader population of Gospel Music songs—not just the songs captured in the sample that is used to estimate the model. In addition, because we have little information concerning the nature of within and between panel (year) differences, it is appropriate to feature a Probit random effects model as opposed to a fixed effects model. We describe fully the Probit panel data model in Equation 4:

Equation 4:
$$(y_{it}|X'_{it}\beta, \alpha_i, \varepsilon_{it}) = y^*_{it} = \alpha_i + \sum_{j=1}^{5} \beta_j X'_{jit} + \varepsilon_{it}.$$

where y_{it} is a discrete dependent variable that assumes the value 1 when a song includes special message lyrics that have the potential to motivate listeners to take action to improve their economic outcomes and 0 otherwise (i.e., $y_{it} = 1$ when the probability of $y^*_{it} > 0$, 0 otherwise); i counts from 1 to 6 (2008 through 2013) representing the number of panels that are in the data set; t counts from 1 to 25 representing the number of observations in each panel in rank order; α_i represents the random effects component of the model (it is common to all panels and is expected to be distributed normally with a 0 mean and a variance of σ^2); β_j represents the estimated parameters for the covariates that have a j count from 1 to 5; X_{jit} represents five exogenous dummy variables (X_{1it} assumes the value 1 if songs include references to economic issues and 0 otherwise; X_{2it} assumes the value 1 if songs are from Great Recession years (2008 and 2009) and 0 otherwise; X_{3it} assumes the value 1 if songs reflect a fast tempi and 0 otherwise; X_{4it} assumes the value 1 if songs are presented in a major musical key and 0 otherwise; and X_{5it} assumes the value 1 if the primary presenters of songs are male and 0 otherwise); ε_{it} is assumed to be a normally distributed error term with a 0 mean and a σ^2 variance. In addition, α_i and ε_{it} are assumed to be uncorrelated and the two are assumed to be uncorrelated with X_{jit}.

Table 2 reflects our hypotheses concerning the arithmetic sign of the estimated parameters for the five covariates:

Table 2.—Hypothesized Signs of Estimated Parameters

Line No.	Covariates	Sign of Estimated Parameters
1	X_{1it} – Song includes Economic Issues	β_{1it} – Contributes positively to Y_{it}
2	X_{2it} – Song is from Great Recession Year	β_{2it} – Contributes positively to Y_{it}
3	X_{3it} – Song reflects fast tempi	β_{3it} – Contributes positively to Y_{it}
4	X_{4it} – Song presented in major musical key	β_{4it} – Contributes positively to Y_{it}
5	X_{5it} – Primary singer is male gender	β_{5it} – Indeterminate

Now we describe the logic of these hypotheses. Logically, one would expect songs that include economic issues to include special messages that motivate listeners to resolve those issues. The Great Recession, because of its harshness, should have motivated songs with special messages for Afrodescendants to fight to improve economic outcomes.

We assume that those in the music industry understand that fast tempi Gospel Music that is presented in a major musical key has the most power to engender positive, upbeat emotions. Consequently, we assume that they will use music configured thusly to carry special messages to improve economic outcomes. Finally, we have no basis for hypothesizing concerning the gender of the primary presenter of songs—although there may be reason to believe that there is a unique statistical relationship to uncover through the estimation process.

VI.   Econometric Results

Table 3 presents three sets of econometric results based on an Ordinary Least Squares (OLS) model, a simple pooled Probit model, and a Probit panel random effects model.[9] Sayrs (1989) recommends using OLS as a starting point for panel data analysis, and we present the OLS model results in column one. In the second column, we present results for the simple pooled Probit model. In the third column, we present the Probit panel data model results. Note that STATA software was used to estimate each of the models: The Newton-Raphson method was used to estimate the simple pooled Probit model, and that the Gaussian-Hermite quadrature method was used to estimate the Probit panel random effects model.

---

[9] Equations are not provided for the OLS and simple pooled Probit models. They would be identical to Equation 4, except that the i subscripts would be eliminated from each of the variables that have them.

Table 3.—OLS, Simple Probit, and Probit Panel Model Estimation Results

Line No.	Covariates/ Statistics	1	2	3
		Estimated Parameters (P-Values)		
		OLS Model	Simple Pooled Probit Model	Panel Data Probit (Random Effects) Model
1	Constant (α_i)	0.1774* (0.003)	-1.0096* (0.025)	
2	Random Effect (α_i)			-1.0097* (0.025)
3	Economic Issues (X_{1it})	0.0608 (0.164)	0.4685 (0.193)	0.4685 (0.193)
4	Recession Year (X_{2it})	0.0494 (0.250)	0.461 (0.196)	0.461 (0.196)
5	BPM (X_{3it})	-0.0021 (0.961)	-0.0562 (0.883)	-0.0562 (0.883)
6	Major Key (X_{4it})	-0.1360* (0.006)	-0.9046* (0.012)	-0.9046* (0.012)
7	Male Artist (X_{5it})	-0.054 (0.242)	-0.3955 (0.295)	-0.3955 (0.295)
8	N	150	150	150
	Adjusted R^2	0.0575		
9	Likelihood Ratio χ^2 Test (5)		11.9	
	Wald χ^2 (5)			10.76
10	Prob > F (5, 144)	0.0185		
	Prob > χ^2 (5)		0.0362	0.0563

*--Significant at least at the 5 percent level.

19

Beginning at row 9 of Table 3, we find that the Adjusted R^2 and the Likelihood Ratio and Wald χ^2 statistics indicate that the models reflect only marginal statistically significant relationships between the dependent variable and the covariates.[10] This is confirmed by the Probability F and χ^2 statistics that appear in row 10 of the table. Turning to the estimated parameters and P-values, all three models reflect two statistically significant parameter estimates at the five percent level: The constant/random effect variable and the coefficient for the variable that assumes the value 1 when songs are presented in a major musical key. However, the arithmetic sign of the latter parameter estimate is inconsistent with our expectations. We hypothesized that songs with special messages would be presented in a major musical key to achieve maximum effect.

In fact, we had hypothesized that the parameter estimates for the first four covariates would reflect a positive sign; only the parameter estimates for the first two covariates are consistent with that reasoning. The parameter estimates on these two covariates (songs including economic issues, and songs appearing on the *Billboard Magazine* Top 25 Gospel Music chart during a Great Recession year (2008 and 2009)), although not statistically significant, imply that they would contribute positively to the predicted probability that the songs included special messages that motivate Afrodescendants to act to improve their economic plight. The arithmetic sign on the parameter estimates for the latter two covariates (songs with over 90 BPM and songs presented in a major musical key) indicate that the existence of such characteristics contribute negatively to the predicted

---

[10]The χ^2 critical value for 5 degrees of freedom is 11.70. Consequently, while the simple pooled Probit model (column 2) passes the test, the panel data Probit model (column 3) does not pass the test. In addition, the Adjusted R^2 for the OLS model (column 1) is very small.

probability that songs include special messages. Note that the beats per minute variable is not statistically significant.

While not statistically significant in any of the three models, the parameter estimate for the final covariate for songs presented by male artists reflects a negative sign. This indicates that male artists' songs do not contribute positively to the predicted probability that songs include special motivating messages. Accordingly, we might hypothesize that female artists may increase the predicted probability that Gospel Music songs will have such special messages— something for which we did not test.

It bears mentioning that, as generally known and as recognized by Arulampalam (1999), the values of the estimated parameters for the simple pooled and panel data Probit models are nearly identical.

Looking specifically at the two statistically significant estimated parameters for the two Probit models, we can provide their marginal contributions to the predicted probability that songs include special motivating messages. The constant/random effects estimated parameter's value of -1.0096/7 means that it reduces the predicted probability that a song will include special messages by about 0.1563. Finally, holding all other covariates fixed at 0, we find that the estimated parameter value for the major key covariate of -0.9046 reduces the predicted probability that songs will include special messages by 0.0278. If we permit all other covariates, which are all dummy variables, to assume the value 1, then the estimated parameter for the major musical key covariate reduces the predicted probability that songs include special messages by 0.0754.

Overall, these results allow us to conclude that the hypothesized relationships between the dependent variable and five covariates are inconsistent with statistical reality. Specifically, the existence of economic issues in songs, the fact that songs appear during a severe economic downturn, and songs' tempi do not contribute significantly and statistically to the predicted probability that songs will include special motivating messages that can stimulate Afrodescendants to take action to improve their economic outcomes. While the major musical key covariate contributes in a statistically significant way to the latter outcome, the arithmetic sign on the estimated parameter for the variable indicates that it contributes negatively not positively to the aforementioned predicted probability. It is also true that the male gender of the artists who sing Gospel Music songs does not contribute materially to the predicted probability that such songs include special motivating lyrics.

VII.   Conclusion

We have used this monograph to construct an argument that, based on history, Gospel Music can be a motive force for change. We augmented that argument with a musical analysis that is based on psychology, which states that music presented at a fast tempi and in a major musical key engenders favorable feelings or emotions. We contended that Gospel Music, which exhibits the just-mentioned characteristics, has the potential to motivate Afrodescendants to take action to improve their economic outcomes when the music contains appropriate messages and is an important part of listeners' environment. Our Gospel Music content analysis of the *Billboard Magazine* Top 25 Gospel Songs for the years 2008 – 2013 revealed that, while economic issues are mentioned often in Gospel Music, only ten of the 150 gospel songs analyzed contained motivating messages designed to help Afrodescendant improve their economic outcomes. Importantly, our content analysis revealed that "faith and prayer only" messages are prevalent in Gospel Music. That is, religious adherents are advised that they need only believe and pray that their problems, including economic problems, will be resolved in order to realize favorable outcomes. The latter revelation was reinforced by our statistical analysis, which showed that our hypotheses about the structure and nature of Gospel Music and its ability to create positive economic change were unfounded.

Economists are the first to explain that, in order to achieve preferred outcomes, effort is required—not just faith and prayer. Quite often, preachers and Gospel Music artists quote an important biblical verse: "Now unto him that is able to do exceeding abundantly above all that we can ask or think," (Ephesians: 3:20). Too often, they fail to complete the verse, which states: "according to the power that worketh in us." In other words, the admonishment is that all things are possible and available when the power of our effort is operationalized. It appears that Gospel Music is guilty of emphasizing the former and not the latter aspects of this scripture.

Consequently, we ask: "Instead of being a motive force for action to improve economic outcomes, does Gospel Music actually serve as a deterrent to such action due to its emphasis on prayer and faith alone?" We hasten to add that Contemporary Gospel Music is not the lone guilty party here. The fact is that, generally speaking and with a few exceptions, most *genres* of Afrodescendant music fail to speak effectively and prevalently to the economic issues and problems that Afrodescendants face during the first and second decades of the 21st century and to relevant solutions. Unlike the message music of the 1960s, we just do not hear popular artists addressing the multifaceted economic issues that Afrodescendants confront the way the great artists of the 1960s tackled Civil Rights and political concerns.

Therefore, we conclude by posing the following questions: "Why does our music fail to fill this gap today? Is the Afrodescendant unemployment rate as high as it is and the Afrodescendant income level as low as it is because we do not use our music to help change these outcomes? Should we not use every tool at our disposal to create improvement in our economic circumstances?" In our view, given its popularity and potential power to effect change, the failure to use Contemporary Gospel Music to create favorable economic outcomes for Afrodescendants is a tragedy.

VIII.   References

Arrow, Kenneth. (1972) "Gifts and Exchanges." *Philosophy and Public Affairs.* Vol. 1, No. 4: 343-62.

Arulampalam, Wiji. (1999) "A Note on Estimated Coefficients in Random Effects Probit Models." *Oxford Bulletin of Economics and Statistics.* Vol. 61, No. 4: 597-602.

Bible Gateway.com. *Holy Bible.* King James Version. Ephesians, Chapter 3. Retrieved from the Internet on February 6, 2014; http://www.biblegateway.com/passage/?search=Ephesians+3&version=KJV.

Billboard Magazine. (2008-2013). "Top 25 Gospel Songs." *Billboard Magazine.* December issues each year. Retrieved from the Internet in December 2012 and 2013; http://www.billboard.com/.

BlackEconomics.org. (2013) *Black Churches and Colleges Scholarships: A Report Brief.* BlackEconomics.org. Seattle; October 1st. Retrieved from the Internet on January 27, 2014; http://www.blackeconomics.org/BELit/BCCS.pdf.

Borghans, Lex, Angela L. Duckworth, James J. Heckman, and Baas ter Weel. (2008) "The Economics and Psychology of Personality Traits." National Bureau of Economic Research Working Paper 13810. Retrieved from the Internet on December 17, 2013; http://www.nber.org/papers/w13810.

Cunha, Flavio and James J. Heckman. (2007) "The Technology of Skill Formation." *American Economic Review.* Vol. 97, No. 2: 31-47.

Dalla Bella, Simone and Isabelle Peretz, Luc Rousseau, and Nathalie Gosselin. (2001) "A Developmental Study of the Affective Value of Tempo and Mode in Music. *Cognition.* Vol. 80: B1-B10.

Dolin, Richard A., Frank Slesnick, and John T. Byrd. (1989) "The Organizational Structures of Church and Orthodoxy." Paper presented at meetings of the Western Economic Association. Lake Tahoe, NV.

Frederick II, Nathaniel. (2009) *Praise God and Do Something: The Role of Black American Gospel Artists as Social Activists, 1945-1960.* A Doctoral Dissertation. Retrieved from the Internet on January 27, 2014; http://gradworks.umi.com/33/74/3374487.html.

Gospel Music Association. (2007) *Christian Gospel: Music that Connects.* Gospel Music Association. Nashville, TN. Retrieved from the Internet on December 18, 2003; http://www.gospelmusic.org/wp-content/uploads/2012/11/GMA-Industry-Overview-2007.pdf.

Greene, William H. (2001) "Fixed and Random Effects in Nonlinear Models." A New York University, Leonard N. Stern School of Business Working Paper." Retrieved from the Internet on February 5, 2014; http://ideas.repec.org/p/ste/nystbu/01-01.html.

Guiso, Luigi, Paola Sapienza, and Luigi Zingales. (2006). "Does Culture Affect Economic Outcomes?" *Journal of Economic Perspectives.* Vol. 20, No. 2: 23-48.

Hunter, Patrick G., E. Glenn Schellenberg, and Ulrich Schimmack. (2008) "Mixed Affective Responses to Music with Conflicting Cues." *Cognition and Emotion.* Vol. 22, No. 2: 327-52.

_____. (2010) "Feelings and Perceptions of Happiness and Sadness Induced by Music: Similarities, Differences, and Mixed Emotions." *Psychology of Aesthetics, Creativity, and the Arts.* Vol. 4, No. 1: 47-56.

Iannaccone, Laurence R. (1998) "Introduction to the Economics of Religion." *Journal of Economic Literature.* Vol. 36, No. 3: 1465-96.

Knack, Stephen and Philip Keefer. (1997) "Does Social Capital Have an Economic Payoff? A Cross-country Investigation." *The Quarterly Journal of Economics.* Vol. 112, No. 4: 1251-88.

Knack, Stephen and Paul Zak. (2001) "Trust and Growth." *Economic Journal.* Vol. 111, No 470: 295-321.

Maddala, G.S. (1987) "Limited Dependent Variable Models Using Panel Data." *The Journal of Human Resources.* Vol. 22, No. 3: 307-38.

Nielsen Company. (2013) *A Look Across Media: The Cross-Platform Report.* The Nielsen Company. New York, NY. Retrieved from the Internet on December 18, 2013; http://www.nielsen.com/us/en/reports/2013/a-look-across-media-the-cross-platform-report-q3-2013.html.

Norris, Michele. (2013) "The Mix: Songs Inspired by the Civil Rights Movement." National Public Radio. Retrieved from the Internet on October 30, 2013; http://www.npr.org/2013/07/09/199105070/the-mix-songs-inspired-by-the-civil-rights-movement.

Rigg, M. (1937) "An Experiment to Determine How Accurately College Students Can Interpret Intended Meaning of Musical Compositions." *Journal of Experimental Psychology.* Vol. 21, No. 2: 223-29.

Roberts, Brent W., Ravenna Helson, and Eva C. Klohnen. (2002) "Personality Development and Growth in Women Across 30 Years: Three Perspectives." *Journal of Personality.* Vol. 70, No. 1: 79-102.

Robinson, Brooks B. (2009) "Black Unemployment and Infotainment." *Journal of Economic Inquiry.* Vol. 47, No. 1: 98-117.

Sayrs, Lois W. (1989) *Pooled Time Series Analysis.* Quantitative Applications in the Social Sciences, Vol. 70. Sage Publications. Thousand Oaks, CA.

Stark, Rodney and William S. Bainbridge. (1985) *The Future of Religion*. University of California Press. Berkeley, CA.

Song Lyrics. (2013) Song lyrics provided in this monograph were confirmed mainly using the following Internet websites: Metrolyrics.com; Sing365.com; Sweetslyrics.com; Songlyrics.com; Lyrics.com; AZlyrics.com; Lyricsmode.com; Lyrcszz.com. Retrieved from the Internet from November 2013 – January 2014.

Statacorp. (2013) STATA/MP Econometric Software. Retrieved from the Internet on February 5, 2014; http://www.stata.com/.

Walker, Wyatt Tee. (1979) *Somebody's Calling My Name: Black Sacred Music and Social Change*. Judson Press. Valley Forge, PA.

Webster, Dwight. (2011) *Gospel Music in the United States of America 1960s-1980s: A Study of the Themes of "Survival," "Elevation," and "Liberation" in a Popular Urban Contemporary Black Folk Mass Music*. A Doctoral Dissertation. Retrieved from the Internet on January 27, 2014; http://gradworks.umi.com/34/59/3459512.html.

BBR:022514